FunThink

12 TOOLS FOR CREATIVE PROBLEM SOLVING

Educator + Parent Edition

researched & written
by C. Ray Frigard
+
designed & illustrated
by Peter Wocken

Treebones Inc
Mound, MN

FunThink: 12 Tools for Creative Problem Solving.

All rights reserved. No part of this book may be reproduced, stored in a retrieval system, or transmitted in any form, by any means, including mechanical, electric, photocopying, recording or otherwise, without written permission of the publisher, unless otherwise stated in this book.

Text © 2007 C Ray Frigard - www.funthink.info
www.treebonesinc.com
Illustrations & Layouts : Peter Wocken - www.peterwocken.com

Copyright © 2007 by C Ray Frigard. All rights reserved.

Treebones Inc.
Mound, Minnesota
www.funthink.info

*To my wife Janet, best
friend & creative partner.*

ACKNOWLEDGEMENTS

I feel blessed to have been the youngest in a family of five children with many adventures and trials that contributed to my early creativity. I've been equally blessed with my own family of four children and two grandchildren, each who has been a great inspiration. We have had our own family adventures with trips in an aging Chevy station wagon (without video), sailing on Lake Superior, and moving about the country with our possessions in tow.

Kind thanks to those who took time to read and edit early drafts: Wendy Elias, Tom Minor, Noreen Watson, Alice Brew, Ed, Shar and Jen Boerema, and my wife Janet.

Also thanks to teachers and students of OSLCS for letting me work out the kinks in their classes.

I owe a special word of thanks to Peter Wocken for his creative graphics and Greg Brew for an enlighten foreword.

foreword: Why Creativity Matters

When I was an instructor at Art Center College of Design, I was charged with preparing students to function in the world of product development. Their place was almost guaranteed if they showed a talent for creative problem solving. The business community of today prizes this aptitude as much as the creative arts fields – this is truly how to think in the 21st century.

The most important aspect of being an effective designer is the ability to consistently provide more than one solution to a problem.

The creative problem solving process simply stated:
- Identify and define the problem
- Generate a number of possible ideas
- Evaluate and select the best solutions
- Implement, test and refine the best solution

This process closely parallels the methodology of the most successful companies in the world. It is based around best ideas, rigorous selection and inclusive refinement. Multiple prototypes are then built to insure the best ideas are captured, developed and shown for selection.

This method for generating solutions works for **any** type of problem. It's not a quick, one-answer approach, but requires the type of training that FunThink advocates. It does, however, offer huge improvements over the traditional "single track development, throw-all-the-money-in-the-universe-to-fix-it" method prevalent in many companies in America.

It has been shown in studies by Americans for the Arts that test scores in all subjects, including SATs, are higher where art and music are taught. As many traditional programs fold under budget pressures, parents and concerned adults need tools like FunThink to foster continued creative growth. As we move from an information economy to one that prizes imagination and problem solving we must seize this moment to educate our children and ourselves.

To me "creativity" and "children" belong together. We can learn from their ability to draw on their imagined environments and creative play in solving problems. The creation of art and craft is one of the few things a student can do that will show tangible progress. Feedback of improvement is automatic and visible.

Visualizing solutions to a problem, then being able to grasp them through drawing or modeling, is one of the most satisfying aspects of being a design professional. The subsequent development and physical manifestation of the object brings a deep, tangible sense of satisfaction – perhaps like our ancestors might have felt when they made the tools that sustained life.

Greg Brew is Director of Industrial Design for Polaris Industries, a Minnesota based manufacturer of all-terrain vehicles, snowmobiles and motorcycles.

He has taught, and was the Associate Chair in the Industrial Design Department at Art Center College of Design, Pasadena, CA., his alma mater. Mr. Brew also taught at the Scuola di Arte Applicata (Turin, Italy) and Instituto Europeo di Design (Turin, Italy). He was a car designer for FIAT Auto SpA., Lancia SpA. and BMW AG.

Table of Contents

- Acknowledgements

- Foreword: Why creativity matters - Greg Brew: Design Educator & ID Director

- Table of Contents

ii   Introduction: Explains purpose and use of FunThink material.

2   #1 Creative Catapult: Use **collaboration** and **brainstorming** to **concept model** a devise to launch a cotton ball four feet.

4   #2 Designer Island: A **concept sketching** exercise using **visual thinking** in organizing an ideal island community.

8   #3 Power Tower: Learn **persistence** when **concept modeling** a tower using toothpicks that will support a pound of clay.

10   #4 Scoop: Introduce **mind mapping** and **springboard research** in outlining a biography of a friend or classmate.

12   #5 Rock Toaster and a Zoo Parade: Rock Toaster is an exercise in **concept sketching** product designs. Zoo Parade is a **concept modeling** challenge in sculpting animals in clay.

14   #6 What Do You Know? Review of **Creativity Tools** and **practice concept sketching**.

16   #7 Money, Brains, and Gravity: **Collaborate** to **concept model** a devise that will transport two pennies at least four feet using only gravity.

volume 01

18	#8 Mine the Mind: Use **journaling**, **visual thinking** and **collaboration** to **mind map** an outline for a Hollywood action movie.
22	#9 Future Think: Choose any of the **creativity tools** to explore original product concepts.
22	#10 Continue Future Think: Experience the **incubation** process between sessions and develop **concept sketches** and **concept models** for presentation of product concepts.
26	#11 "Houston": The Apollo 13 mission of 1970 taught the world the power of **Creative Problem Solving** in bringing the astronauts home safely. The challenge is to deliver a "payload" by **concept modeling** as many methods as possible.
30	#12 Pile of Junk: Choose any of the **creativity tools** to take on real world problems. " To invent you need a good imagination and a pile of junk." Thomas Edison
32	#13 Uncle Horatio's Gift: **Design** the perfect cabin retreat on beautiful Lake Tahoe.
36	#14 Reflection and a Final Challenge: Author's **creative process** and student challenge.
40	FunThink Afterword
41	Worksheet #1 for "Designer Island"
43	Worksheet #2 for "Scoop"
45	Worksheets #3 - #7 for "What Do You Know?"

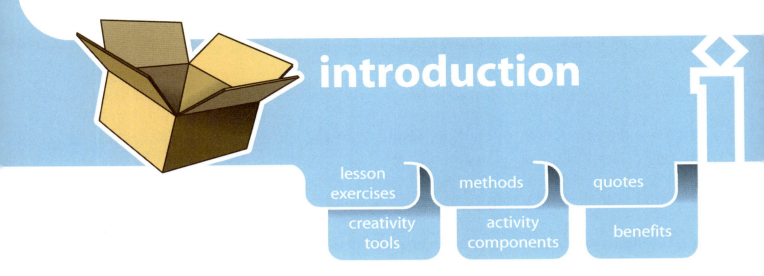

INTRODUCTION

It seems everywhere we turn these days there is a call for innovation, be it in alternative power, health care, transportation, government, or education to name just a few. The purpose of this curriculum is to develop **creative problem solving skills** and **"thinking tools"** that are necessary in answering the call for innovative thinking. No special skills are needed to be successful in the FunThink activities, which are designed to draw out knowledge and innate skills as well as spark original thought and creative problem solving.

It is rather ironic that such an important matter as innovation can be approached with a **sense of playfulness**. Research in creativity has shown that we are much more creative when not under stress to perform. Creativity is an **engaging experience** where the process is rewarding in itself; we create for the love of it, sort of like getting to scratch an itch. There are **no right or wrong answers** in the hands-on FunThink activities. They are designed to allow for freedom of expression, taking risks, and the opportunity to **"think outside the box"** while sneakily teaching the creative problem solving process.

QUOTES

"There has never been a time in history when the character of human imagination wasn't important…But it has never been more important than now. Therefore, thinking about how we stimulate positive imaginations is of the utmost importance."
Thomas Friedman *The World is Flat*

"There is something about the fluid habits of mind fostered by play that inventors value and continue to use as part of their working lives."
Lemelson Center for the Study of Invention and Innovation *Invention Manual*

"Creativity is a skill. It is not something mystical available only to a few. It can be learned by anyone. Everyone possesses an innate capacity for creativity."
James M. Higgins *101 Creative Problem Solving Techniques*

Problem solving in the classroom is generally based on knowledge and information where there is only one correct answer, as in solving a math or physics problem or answering a history question. **Creative Problem Solving** draws not only on knowledge but involves the imagination that fosters original solutions. Applying creativity to problem solving is vital in developing innovative products in business or solving community issues like safety, housing and education.

Through using the 12 creativity tools in solving the FunThink challenges students learn to exercise their **imagination** and creative problem solving skills. These critical skills will enrich their personal, work, and community life.

sketchbook

color study

finished product

stages of an idea from begining to end

LESSON EXERCISES

A. Activity Introduction
- **Background** information on the activity.
- **Prompts** that can be offered to help in meeting success.
- **Examples** of student work.
- Pertinent **quotes** by creative people.

B. Activity Format
- The **lesson title** expresses the activity theme.
- The **materials** used in solving the challenge. (One set of materials per collaborative team unless otherwise noted)
- The **suggested time** for each segment of the activity.
- The **creativity tools** used in solving the challenge.
- The **objective statement** defines the goal.
- The **challenge scenario** is a descriptive statement that helps visualize the problem to be solved.
- The last segment is the **demonstration/presentation** of the solution to the challenge.

C. Additional Comments
- Balancing challenge and accomplishment is important for a positive experience. **Meeting success** is more important than getting it "right"; experiencing the process is the goal.
- When collaboration is called for, two people work together. In a **home school setting** the teacher can be a collaborator or the student can work alone.
- Using inexpensive common material keeps the cost down but also helps to maintain the **focus on ideas** and not on making something beautiful.
- When instructing a large class it is helpful to sort the **materials** into individual zip-lock baggies before class.
- The models are scaled to be **easily constructed** on a desktop or kitchen table.
- The complete activity is on one page with easy to follow **concise directions**.
- Instructors will probably notice that some students are **more comfortable** in sketching while others like modeling and yet others like the writing challenges.
- To signify that this is a **special** time adding background music or setting out artwork or posters etc can contribute to a relaxed environment.
- In a classroom setting it is important that the instructor acknowledge each student's solution in a **non-threatening** way by either reviewing them at their desk, or asking them to present to the class from their desk, or having them present from the front of the class. As **confidence** grows they will enjoy presenting their solutions to the challenges.
- Only **copying** of the handout material is permitted.

METHODS, TOOLS, COMPONENTS AND BENEFITS

The main focus of FunThink is on the following **four steps** of the creative problem solving (CPS) process.

1- <u>Recognize and **define** the problem to be solved</u>.
   Each session opens with a challenge scenario that states the problem to be solved. The problem should be **clearly** identified before proceeding.

2- <u>**Generate** a number of potential solutions</u> (Divergent)
   While each session is designed to be challenging, success is important. It is hard to think of failure as a positive attribute but it is the **engine** that can drive innovation. As an example Thomas Edison "failed" more than 1000 times before he succeeded in finding the correct material for the light bulb. Likewise in FunThink generating a number of possible solutions is part of the learning process.

3- <u>**Evaluate** and select best solution</u> (Convergent)
   Once generated, ideas need to be evaluated to find the **best** solution.

4- <u>**Implement** and present best solution</u>
   It must be stressed again that the goal is to capture ideas and not a perfect sketch, exquisite prose, a beautiful model or award-winning art. **All solutions** have value when they are the result of an individual's creative process. Implementation and demonstration of the solution is the final step in CPS.

QUOTES

I made 5,127 prototypes of my vacuum before I got it right. There were 5,126 failures. But I learned from each one. That's how I came up with a solution. So I don't mind failure. I've always thought that schoolchildren should be marked by the number of failures they've had.
Sir James Dyson, *Inventor of the best selling vacuum in the U.S., Fast Company May 2007*

Anyone who has never made a mistake has never tried anything new.
Albert Einstein

CREATIVITY TOOLS

The following definitions are purposely concise to aid in retention and are used throughout the course for explanation and review of the creativity "tools".

1- **Creative Problem Solving** (CPS): A process for generating creative solutions.
   a. **Define** the problem or goal.
   b. **Generate** a number of possible solutions.
   c. **Evaluate** and select the best solution.
   d. **Implement** and demonstrate or present the best solution.

2- **Brainstorming**: Generate creative ways to meet a goal or solve a problem.

3- **Visual Thinking**: Use the "mind's eye" to work on problems in your head.

4- **Concept Sketching**: Use simple sketches to manipulate ideas on paper.

5- **Concept Modeling**: Use simple model materials to explore concepts.

6- **Journaling**: Record experiences/information to be used later in problem solving.

7- **Mind Mapping**: A graphic method of organizing information.

8- **Collaboration**: Work with others to generate ideas and problem solve.

9- **Incubation**: Allowing the subconscious to work on problems; "sleep on it".

10- **Springboard Research**: Background information used to problem solve.

11- **Persistence**: Continue to press on in spite of difficulty.

12- **Practice**: Repeated activity to gain and maintain a skill.

viii
ACTIVITY COMPONENTS

- Drawing
- Model making
- Engineering
- Creative writing
- Designing
- Reporting
- Research
- Testing
- Evaluation
- Planning
- Imagination
- Architecture
- Landscaping
- Communication
- Presentation
- Organization
- Demonstration
- Invention

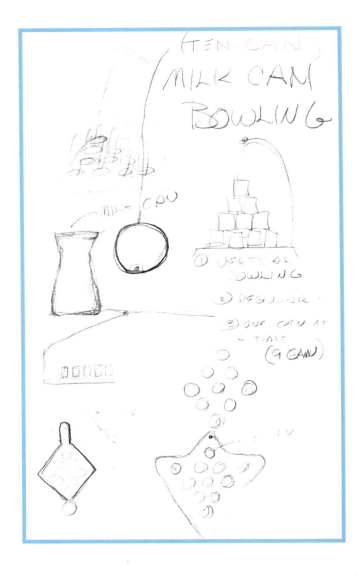

stages of an idea from beginning to end

QUOTES

Work brings inspiration if inspiration is not discernible in the beginning.
Igor Stravinsky, *Composer*

If we did things we are capable of, we would literally astound ourselves.
Thomas Alva Edison

...Einstein was, in a way, returning to the conceptual world of childhood: the search for basic understandings unhampered by conventional delineations of a question. Indeed, the very puzzles that he first pursued as a youth....later fueled his most innovative scientific work.
Howard Gardener, *Creating Minds*

BENEFITS

- <u>Creativity</u>: Students that have taken classes in creativity claim they "feel" more creative. Consequently, they actually become more creative, showing that their innate creativity can be **drawn out**.
- <u>Cooperation</u>: A very important ingredient for innovation in business is the ability to brainstorm and **work with others** in the creative problem solving process.
- <u>Success</u>: Anyone can have success when there are no right or wrong answers. The goal is to create a non-threatening environment where there is **freedom** to try out ideas and take risks, which is essential in innovation.
- <u>Focus</u>: Its easy to focus when we are exercising our imaginations and having a **good time**. Learning to focus is important in problem solving.
- <u>Retention</u>: Studies show that retention rate is higher when involved in **hands-on** learning.
- <u>Originality</u>: Each activity encourages original thinking. The idea of coming up with an original concept is new to many people and gives them a sense of being **special**, which of course they are.
- <u>Stress relief</u>: Psychologists tell us that we are more creative when not under pressure to perform. Being **creative** is also a good stress reliever.
- <u>Transference of CPS</u>: Learning creative problem solving will **serve** children and adults well in areas of education, social, and future work life.
- <u>Discover interests/talents</u>: Through using the creativity tools individuals may find new areas of **interest** in sketching, model building, art, etc.

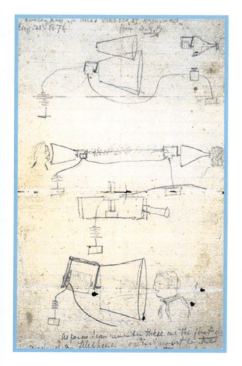

sketch from Alexander Graham Bell, telephone inventor

creative catapult

INTRODUCTION

The first few lessons get right into **Creative Problem Solving** (CPS) without much explanation of the process. The idea is to get students actively engaged in the use of the **Creativity Tools** so they come to an understanding of the concepts through hands-on application.

This might be the first opportunity that they are allowed to express themselves in such an **open-ended manner**. Teachers can expect a great deal of activity, experimentation, and vocal excitement.

Students seem to collaborate naturally and work well together when a challenge is presented and a **common goal** is understood. In this activity they will **collaborate** with one other person.

This activity will emphasize **concept modeling**. Through the use of **simple model materials** they will focus more on creative problem solving and spend less time worrying about what looks good. This teaches that solutions are what is important.

The **main rule** for all FunThink activities is to use **only** the materials provided. In this activity paper or cotton balls are the **only** things that can be catapulted.

The **process** is more important than the product in all activities and having a positive experience is one of the main goals so teachers should feel free to offer a **prompt** if a student is stuck.

Supplemental information on **Brainstorming** and **Collaboration**:
• 101 Creative Problem Solving Techniques *James M. Higgins*

QUOTES

"When asked what inspired them to **become inventors**, many adults tell stories about playing as children. Among inventors' most frequently cited childhood play experiences are: mechanical **tinkering**, **fiddling** with construction toys, **reflecting** in and about nature, and **drawing** or engaging in other forms of visual **modeling**."
Lemelson Center for the Study of Invention and Innovation *Invention Manual*

"By having (students) collaborate in activities with classmates whose minds are very different from their own, we can foster more respect for the differences."
Mel Levine *A Mind at a Time*

LESSON

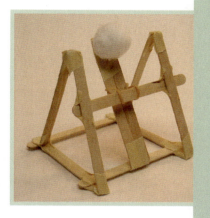

MATERIALS
1. 1" cotton ball or paper wad
2. (3) #16 or #18 rubber bands
3. (1) 12" length ¾" or 1" masking tape.
   (have extra tape to hand out if needed)
4. 12 craft sticks.

CREATIVITY TOOLS
1. Collaboration
2. Brainstorming
3. Concept Modeling

TIME
1. Challenge explanation. 5 min.
2. Team concept modeling and build of final test catapult. 30 min.
3. Concept Presentation. 15 min.

OBJECTIVE
1. Introduce simple modeling materials used in problem solving.

CHALLENGE
"You are a creative thinker in 12th century Europe. The king's army field commander approaches you for help to come up with a means to knock down castle walls in siege warfare.

Collaborate with another great thinker and **brainstorm** as many solutions as possible using the materials provided. From what you have learned in your **concept models**, build a final test catapult that will demonstrate your best solution to the challenge by launching the cotton ball at least 4 feet." (Remind students **only** cotton balls or paper can be launched. For additional challenges try to land the cotton ball in a cup.)

designer island

INTRODUCTION

We are all gifted with **Visual Thinking**, the ability to see things in our **"mind's eye"**. When we are read to we create complex mental images that follow the story line. We can use this amazing power to visually **manipulate** things in our mind to solve problems.

Most students will be able to visualize the house, door and window exercise on the following lesson page. If someone does not see the image they are **not defective** only that they probably weren't tuned into the description. It is suggested to move on to the challenge statement, which is the main point of the activity.

Instructors may **hand out** the Designer Island Development Plan (*Page 41)* or **write** the community requirements on the board.

Depending upon experience, students will have different sketching abilities. Stress that **everyone** is capable of **Concept Sketching**, which is **all about ideas** and not expertise in drawing a beautiful picture. In all FunThink activities sketching is used to get ideas out of the head and down on paper where they can be manipulated. Sketching out our ideas can often communicate our thoughts better than verbalizing them.

Supplemental information on **Sketching** and **Visual Thinking**:
- The Usborne Complete Book of Drawing *Usborne*
- Thinking Visually *Robert H. McKim*

QUOTES

"I shut my eyes so I can see"
Paul Gauguin *Artist*

"While creativity is the natural propensity of human being-ness, creativity can be enhanced and also stifled. The creative personality can be developed and also thwarted."
Dr. Jane Piirto *Understanding Creativity*

LESSON 5

MATERIALS
1- (1) Basic set of colored pencils, markers, or crayons. (Optional)
2- (1) Designer Island Development Plan (page 41)
3- (1) 11"x17" sheet white copy paper or comparable

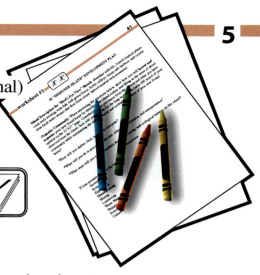

CREATIVITY TOOLS
1- Visual Thinking
2- Concept Sketching

TIME
1- Read **visual thinking** exercise, **challenge** statement, and then hand out and read the **Designer Island Development Plan**. 10 min.
2- As if **looking down** from above, children **sketch** their Designer Island from the description in the challenge statement. They must then **organize** a community that will meet their needs for the next 100 years. 25 min.
3- **Share** results in the time remaining. 15 min.

OBJECTIVE
Help student become aware of their **innate** visual thinking capacity. Without any special training they already know how to express their ideas through concept sketching.

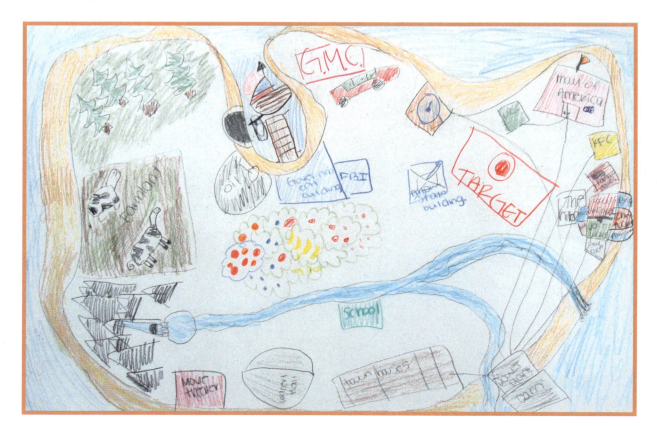

6

VISUAL THINKING

"Close your eyes and try to **imagine** the front of a house with a door and a window on each side. Now remove the door and move the window on the left to where the door was. Now put the door where the window on the left was.

(Pause) Open your eyes. Were some of you able to see the house in your mind? This is an example of **visual thinking** showing that you can **move things** around in your mind. If you didn't get an image, you are not defective, it's just that this description may not have worked for you."

CHALLENGE

"To your own amazement, you have led a small scientific research team in building a **time machine** that actually works! For your first trip you gather several hundred family members, friends, and fellow researchers to travel ahead in time 100 years where you see many fantastic innovations for a better life. In trying to return back to the present, you **mistakenly** go back 1000 years and land on a beautiful, pristine uninhabited island in the Pacific Ocean. The bad news is that you are stuck in this place in time because your machine was **destroyed** upon arrival. However, the island has everything you need to sustain life: abundant wild life; fruited tropical plants; coral reefs teeming with fish; lush, green forest; fertile valleys; storm-safe harbors; and crystal-clear fresh water streams that flow from cloud-haloed mineral rich mountains. Feeling responsible, you try to make the best of things by concept sketching a **plan** for settling in your new home."

power tower 3

INTRODUCTION

While exploring solutions for their "Power Tower" most students will **naturally follow** the CPS (Creative Problem Solving) process. This four-step process is used in company research and development groups and is the foundation of all successful problem solutions.

The CPS steps can be written on the board periodically as a reminder:
1- Recognize and **define** the problem to be solved.
2- **Generate** a number of potential solutions.
3- **Evaluate** and select best solution.
4- **Implement** and demonstrate best solution.

Students collaborate in 2-person teams and are encouraged to try **several approaches** to solve the problem.

Failure is an **important motivator** in CPS and is totally acceptable. Students may need to be encouraged to try something different again and again reminding them that Edison tried hundreds of tests before he succeeded with the first light bulb. Successful innovation is often found through the door of "failure."

Supplemental information on **Creative Problem Solving**:
• Applied Imagination *Alex F. Osborn*

QUOTES

"All sorts of things can happen when you're open to new ideas and playing around with things."
Stephanie Kwolek *Inventor of Kevlar*

" Don't fear mistakes; there are none".
Miles Davis *Musician*

LESSON

MATERIALS
1- (20-25) Wooden "flat" toothpicks. 1 box=750
2- ¼ of a stick of clay. (Four sticks to a package)
3- One unopened package of clay (12oz to 16oz each) to test towers.

CREATIVITY TOOLS
1- CPS
2- Concept Modeling
3- Collaboration

TIME
1- Challenge explanation: 5 min.
2- Build Concept Models. Pick the best idea for the weight test: 30 min.
3- Students conduct weight test by placing one package of clay on the towers (for fun add additional weight if time permits):15 min.

OBJECTIVE
The abstract nature of the materials will lead students into trying unconventional approaches to the problem, thus drawing them into **open-ended thinking**.

CHALLENGE
"Your small construction company must prove to the local city inspector that you have the capability to take on a major engineering project in town. Even though the materials you are given to build a model are only toothpicks and clay, you can demonstrate your **innovative thinking** by building a tower platform **one toothpick high** that can hold a minimum weight of one package of clay. Take about 20 minutes to explore different configurations. Then build your best design for the final weight test."

NOTE: Models should be tested on a flat level surface. If models are built on a sloped desktop, prop up the lid to be level to the floor. Models should be built on a piece of paper so they can be moved easily if needed.

scoop

INTRODUCTION

In Scoop students are introduced to **Mind Mapping**, which is an effective and creative way to generate ideas and record information. Because of its graphic nature it is easy to visualize and group information, add and move things around.

Being interviewed allows students to talk about themselves as well as do **Springboard Research** on others. Springboard research is needed to gather background information for writing a newspaper article.

This activity helps to **reinforce** note taking. They will need to **listen** closely for pertinent information, and then use **keywords** as notes on their mind map. Next they **transpose** their notes into a written article that can be orally presented.

Some simple rules in mind mapping:
1- Start with the **main idea** in the center box, in this case a name. The eight **subtopics** are circled and connected with a line to the central idea.
2- **Keywords** of new information branch out on lines from each subtopic.
3- All words should be **printed** (for easy recall) and placed on their own line.
4- Maps are meant to look **free form**.
5- Optional: It can be suggested to use small **images** (sketches) in place of words as a method of recall, like a palm tree representing a trip to Disney World in Florida. Colors can be used to further delineate the subtopics, aiding recall and adding creative flare.

More information on **Mind Mapping**:
- Use Both Sides of Your Brain, *Tony Buzan*
- Mapping Inner Space, *Nancy Margulies*
- The Mind Map Book, *Tony Buzan*

LESSON 11

MATERIALS
1- Scoop interview form (page 43)

CREATIVITY TOOLS
1- Mind Mapping
2- Springboard Research

TIME
1- Challenge explanation. 5 minutes
2- Interviewing and recording information on the Mind Map. 15 minutes
3- Write article. 15 minutes
4- Read and/or post articles in time left. 15 minutes

OBJECTIVE
Learning to listen, share and record information about each other; will help students become better collaborators.

CHALLENGE
"You are an aspiring rookie reporter for the Daily Times. Your first assignment is to do **springboard research** by interviewing a totally unique individual. To make sure you get the "scoop" on this person, you ask probing, insightful questions from your scoop interview form.

From this hot scoop you must put together a concise, but informative, column and get it to the editor before press time. Use the scoop interview form and **mind map** outline to ask and record information about the person. From the information gathered on your mind map write a concise article using fewer than 150 words."

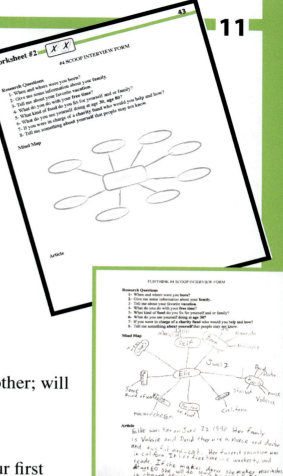

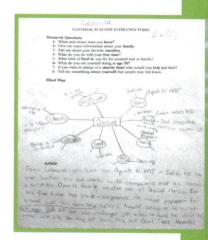

QUOTES

"A mind once stretched by a new idea never regains its original dimensions".
Oliver Wendell Holmes *Supreme Court justice*

"Mapping enables us to express our understanding as we take in and transform information into knowledge and wisdom."
Nancy Margulies *Mapping Inner Space*

rock toaster & zoo parade

INTRODUCTION

It is important for students to understand that they <u>already</u> have a wealth of knowledge and capabilities that can be used in CPS. By connecting two **existing** ideas that they know about it is possible to create new product concepts. A perfect example of this convergence of ideas is the automobile, where inventors joined the carriage or wagon with an existing mechanical device or motor to drive the wheels.

In the **Rock Toaster** exercise on the following lesson page, the unrelated <u>object</u> list is meant as a catalyst to **Concept Sketch** "out of the box" imaginative solutions to the students' <u>product list</u> in the challenge statement.

In **Zoo Parade** they develop **Concept Models** by clay modeling known objects quickly, which helps them to focus on what is **essential** in the object and not the perfection of the appearance. Besides just being fun and therapeutic, clay has an amorphous fluid nature that helps students concept model quickly, like sketching in 3-D. This medium is still used to develop full sized models in car, snowmobile, and toy company design studios.

These activities may take two class periods.

Supplemental information on **Concept Sketching** and **Concept Modeling**:
• Cracking Creativity *Mickael Michalko*

QUOTES

"I don't draw a line between play and work."
Newman Darby *sailboard inventor*

"Creativity is God's gift to us, using our creativity is our gift back to God."
Julia Cameron *The Artist Way*

LESSON

13

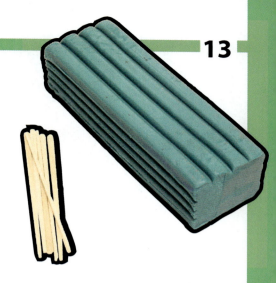

MATERIALS
1- (2) Sheets sketch paper.
2- (1) 3oz or 4oz clay stick per student.
3- (6) Toothpicks per student.

CREATIVITY TOOLS
1- Concept Sketching
2- Concept Modeling

TIME
1- Write product and object list on the board and read challenge explanation: 5 min.
2- "Rock Toaster": Concept Sketching. 15 - 30 min.
3- "Zoo Parade": Concept Modeling. 15 -30 min.
4- Each student tallies how many animals they were able to model in the time allowed and also present their unique design concept. 15 min.

OBJECTIVE
Help students gain a fresh perspective on ordinary things through sketching and modeling.

CHALLENGE
"In the Rock Toaster challenge you will sharpen your sketching skills by combining one item from the following **PRODUCT LIST** with one from the **OBJECT LIST** and Concept Sketch a new product design. This is meant to inspire imaginative "out of the box" thinking that can lead to new product concepts. Do as many product ideas as time allows.

Example: what would a rock toaster look like? Remember there are no right or wrong answers and you are more creative when you are having fun!"

PRODUCT LIST: coffee cup, easy chair, slippers, radio, hat, toaster, lamp, guitar, skateboard, and backpack.
OBJECT LIST: rock, flower, tree, cloud, rocket, lion, bird, elephant, truck, and car.

"In Zoo Parade you must **Concept Model** as many animals as you can in the time allowed. The models can be small but must be recognizable."

what do you know? 6

INTRODUCTION

Sketch is defined as "a rough unfinished drawing or version of any creative work." So a **Concept Sketch** is a rough (quick) drawing that expresses an idea.

Sketching is probably the most important tool for the creative thinker. What comes as natural as running and jumping when we are young often turns into anxious inhibition when we get older. **Concept sketching** is not about creating great art but drawing well enough to communicate an idea to others. It should be required along with the 3Rs. We are only touching the surface of this important tool, but it is a start. The Edwards' books below are great supplements on the importance of drawing in the development of critical-thinking and problem solving. Of course, what can be gained without **Practice**? Practice naturally goes with this sketching activity.

Remind students to keep their hand and forearm loose like waving to someone. Encourage free association doodling. Its fun to just move the pencil around on the page making squiggles and shapes and see what turns up on the paper.

- **Dr. Betty Edwards** *Drawing on the Right Side of the Brain* and *Drawing on the Artist Within*
- Good beginning books on drawing: *The Usborne Complete Book of Drawing* and **Wendon Blake** *Starting to Draw*

QUOTES

"No skill, whether it be skill in basketball, in playing the cello or in thinking, can be acquired by passive reading; skills can be acquired only by active and informed experience….requires sustained and repeated effort."
Robert H. McKim *Thinking Visually*

"…visual, perceptual skills are enhanced by training, just as the verbal, analytic skills benefit by education. Learning to see and draw is a very efficient way to train the visual system, just as learning to read and write can efficiently train the verbal system."
Dr. Betty Edwards *Drawing on the Artist Within*

LESSON 15

MATERIALS
1- Sketch paper
2- Review page and practice sheets on sketching (pages 45-53)

CREATIVITY TOOLS
1- Practice
2- Concept Sketching

TIME
1- Challenge explanation and go through creativity tool review. 10 min.
2- Sketching exercises 40 min.

OBJECTIVE
Students are introduced to all of the creativity tools and focus on two of the most important ones, sketching and practice.

CHALLENGE
"In the past weeks you have had many challenges, from engineering towers and inventing product, to sculpting animals and sketching islands. You have learned many of the tools for creative thinking. Now you get to practice one of the most important tools….drum roll……**Practice!**

First review the 12 creativity tools used in problem solving. Even though you haven't been introduced to all the tools, try matching the creativity tool with the correct definitions on the review page.

Next practice your **Concept Sketching** skills by duplicating the drawings in the open squares on the hand out sheets. These are just warm-up exercises so stay loose and have fun!"

INTRODUCTION

Unlike a problem in algebra where there is only one correct answer, in CPS there can be numerous good solutions. In this activity students seem to naturally follow the **CPS process**. They will first come to understand and **define** the problem. The limited amount of materials actually is a benefit in helping them focus on the problem, simply to transport (carry) the 2 pennies using only the materials provided a minimum distance on the floor of 4 feet.

When students make the connection between spools as wheels and gravity as "motor", most will sense that AH! HAH! feeling. This experience will engage their imagination, and **generate** a number of possible solutions.

Through **evaluating** their various ideas they will choose the best solution. At this point they are usually excited to show off (**implement and demonstrate**) their unique solutions. The goal is to go at least 4 feet, but, of course, a contest can follow to see who can go the furthest distance.

Concept Modeling in a collaborative, non-threatening, and supportive environment will make it easier for individuals to take the risk necessary for CPS. Remind students that failure is proof that they are trying something new, and **original thinking** is one of the main goals in FunThink activities.

QUOTES

"'Creativity is the only American competitive advantage left.' John G. Young, former CEO, Hewlett-Packard. 'For individuals, the development of creative problem-solving skills is a necessity, not a luxury.'"
James M. Higgins *101 Creative Problem Solving Techniques*

"Every child is an artist. The problem is how to remain an artist once he grows up."
Pablo Picasso *Artist*

LESSON

17

MATERIALS
1- (2) Straws, (2) spools, (2) pennies
2- (4) Craft sticks
3- 12" length of ¾" tape. Hand out extra tape as needed.
4- (2) 8 ½"x11" paper (hint: launch ramp)

CREATIVITY TOOLS
1- Brainstorming
2- Collaboration
3- Concept Modeling

TIME
1- Challenge explanation. 5 min.
2- Brainstorm and test a number of ideas. 25 min.
3- Demonstrate to class best solution.
   (Possible contest for distance) 20 min.

OBJECTIVE
Students learn to use materials at hand to explore solutions through brainstorming and collaboration.

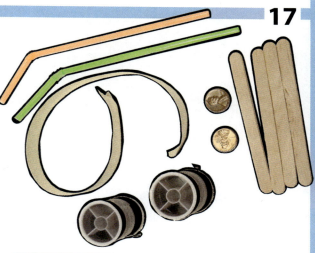

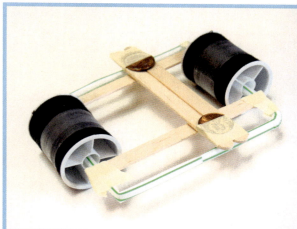

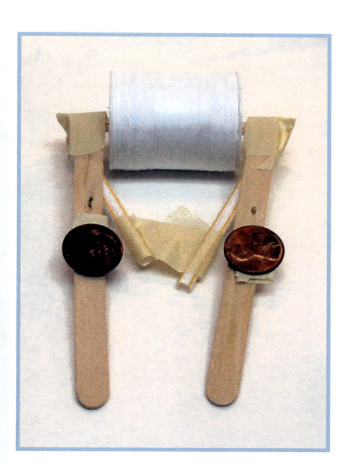

CHALLENGE
"Money, brains, and gravity are all that you need to solve this engineering feat. Your challenge is to discover the best means to **transport** two (2) pennies at least a **distance of 4 feet** along the floor by using only the **materials given**. Take 25 minutes to collaborate and brainstorm as many ideas as possible then build your best model. In the last 20 minutes there will be a test run for the distance of 4 feet and to see who goes the furthest."

INTRODUCTION

Try to bring students to a sense of **calm** before starting the first challenge. Peaceful music in the background might help. Wait for complete silence before opening with the warm-up activities.

Creativity doesn't happen in a vacuum. Some form of inspiration is needed to ignite the flames of imagination. In the two warm-up activities the student is given a brief description of a city and jungle setting. From this **starter broth** they add their own ingredients from past experiences and **Visual Thinking** to create original work.

Review with students the concept of **Journaling**. Encourage them to record their thoughts and experiences on a regular basis. This is a discipline that helps build confidence in creative writing. In this case they are journaling a virtual trip, one created in their imagination.

Remind students of the basic rules and benefits in **Brainstorming**.
- 1- Be open to all ideas **without** judgment.
- 2- **Adding** to other people's ideas is encouraged.
- 3- The **more** ideas generated, better the chances of getting great ideas.
- 4- More ideas can be generated in less time through **collaborative** brainstorming.
- 5- **Evaluate** and choose the best ideas.

QUOTES

"…creativity is linked to work. We have to generate a lot of writing to generate good writing."
Jack Heffron *The Writer's Idea Workshop*

"The future belongs to a very different kind of person with a very different kind of mind…creators and empathizers, pattern recognizers, and meaning makers…artists, inventors, designers, storytellers, caregivers, consolers, big picture thinkers. We are moving from the Information Age to the Conceptual Age."
Daniel H. Pink *A Whole New Mind*

(*continued from previous page*)

The "Rescue from the Amazon" exercise will give students another opportunity to experience the benefits of **Mind Mapping** and **Collaboration**. The six acts on the mind map serve as an outline for students to add creative detail. Emphasize that each act needs to have a <u>major problem</u> with a <u>resolution</u> before going on to the next act.

Write the mind-map on the blackboard or overhead projector.

RESCUE FROM THE AMAZON
    NYC
    Airport
    Plane
    Crash
    Rescue
    Conclusion

LESSON

MATERIALS
    1- Pencil and paper

CREATIVITY TOOLS
    1- Visual Thinking
    2- Journaling
    3- Collaboration
    4- Brainstorming
    5- Mind Mapping

TIME
Read challange #1 and #2 in the time noted on the next page.

OBJECTIVE
Students learn that some form of inspiration or stimulus is needed to spark their imagination in order to create original ideas. In this case, listening to the city and jungle senario.

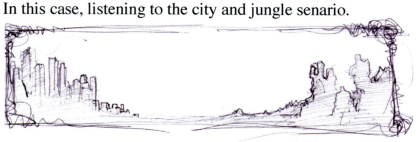

#1 CHALLENGE

"While sitting at your favorite fast food restaurant you peel off the contest label on your large soft drink and realize you have won a free **virtual trip for you** and your family (or friend) to New York City. Now, to prepare for this fantastic trip close your eyes, relax and try to **visualize** what a large, noisy city would be like (pause). As you walk around the bustling city streets, packed with people and traffic, look around at the shop windows and the tall buildings. There are vendors on the street corners selling hotdogs and pretzels from their pushcarts, and people are carrying shopping bags and talking on their cell phones as they hustle along (pause). Now open your eyes and write a few sentences about your virtual trip. What images came to mind as you walked the streets of New York City. Use words that describe the sounds, smells, taste, size and color of things.
<u>You have just 5 minutes.</u>"

"Again, close your eyes, relax, and take a deep breath. Now for a totally **different experience** you fly into the middle of the Amazon jungle. You land on a very small landing strip cut out of the dense rain forest. You step out of the single engine plane and into a totally different world from that of a busy city. There is the sound of a waterfall in the distance. A vividly colored bird that lands in the lush jungle foliage catches your eye. You are warmly greeted by a small group of mahogany-skinned people. You have a feeling this is going to be something to write home about (pause).

Open your eyes and write in your virtual journal, using descriptive words, how you felt and what you saw as you looked around in those first moments. Remember this is your virtual trip so let your imagination run free.

<u>You have just 5 minutes</u>."
#1 Presentation: Students read their favorite journal image. <u>10 minutes</u>

QUOTES

"The way you put everything together-how you arrange the elements-is the design. Its how you translate your concept into visual form."
Robin Landa - *Thinking Creatively*

"But to create an enhanced effect called enrichment, the learning and memory must be new (novel), tough, and worthwhile."
Eric Jensen- *Enriching the Brain*

#2 CHALLENGE
"Now that your imagination is warmed up, you will break into groups of two and brainstorm ideas for an adventure story called "Rescue from the Amazon." **Brainstorming** groups like these collaborate and share ideas to write TV and movie scripts. Pretend your team is about to write the next great action movie. You will use **mind mapping** to record the outline of the story. Mind mapping is a **quick way** to record and organize your ideas. It also allows you to see the **whole story** at once and it is easy to add and **move ideas** around. The mind map on the board (or hand out sheet) shows the 6 acts in the story. Your challenge is to add ideas to each of the circled acts as an outline to write a movie script.

The **story opens** with you and your family or friend packing for your trip to the Amazon jungle. Think of things that will make the story exciting or tense like losing your tickets but finding them in the trash at the last minute, or having a flat tire on the way to the airport. In each of the acts write something that is a **major problem** but then gets **resolved** before the next act. In the conclusion act write about how the main characters changed or were affected by what they experienced."

You have just 20 Minutes
#2 Presentation: A student from each group reads their story outline. 10 minutes

future think 9 & 10

INTRODUCTION

Students work **individually** in both sessions. In session #9 students will choose **one or more items** of interest from the product list. They will do **Springboard Research** on their item by looking through magazines. They can then try out some of their new ideas by generating **Concept Sketches** and **Concept Models**. At the end of this first session, explain the concept of **Incubation** as an opportunity for the subconscious to work on their problems.

Often by researching or thinking about their project before going to sleep **new ideas** will come to mind in the following days. Between now and the next session they should think about their project and **record** any new thoughts and bring them to the next session.

In Session #10 students will develop a final Concept Sketch and/or Concept Model of their best idea. Their ideas can be **presented** to the class one at a time or displayed on a table for others to see.

QUOTES

"In the United States…the intellectual property sectors, whose value depends on their ability to generate new ideas rather than to manufacture commodities, are now the most powerful element in the US economy."
Daniel H. Pink *A Whole New Mind*

"Imagination is more important than Knowledge. For while knowledge defines all we currently know and understand, imagination points to all we might yet discover and create."
Albert Einstein

LESSON 23

MATERIALS
1- (1) 3oz or 4oz clay stick
2- Sketch paper
3- (10) Toothpicks
4- (5) Craft sticks
5- Card stock / poster board, tape, and scissors at central location. Used as needed.

REFERENCE MATERIALS
1- Good variety of "used" magazines that can be cut up for springboard research.

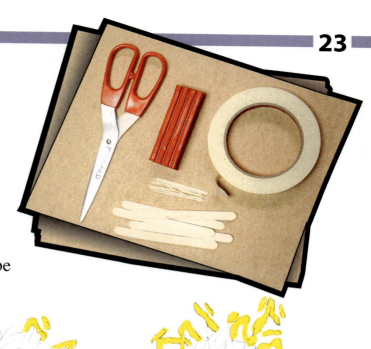

CREATIVITY TOOLS
1- CPS
2- Springboard Research
3- Visual Thinking
4- Concept Sketching
5- Concept Modeling
6- Incubation

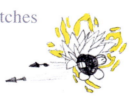

sci-fi movie monster sketches

TIME
Class #9
1- Challenge explanation: 10 min.
2- Springboard Research, Concept Sketches, and Concept Modeling: 40 min.

Class #10
1- Students sketch and/or model their best solutions: 30 min.
2- Class presentation: individually or displayed as a group: 20 min.

OBJECTIVE
Practice using most of the creativity tools **together** to produce product concepts.

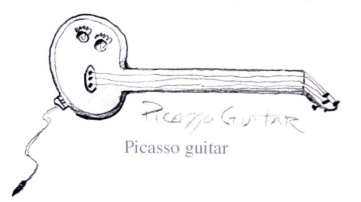

Picasso guitar

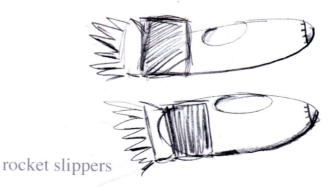

rocket slippers

CHALLENGE
"A major client comes to the design firm where you are working, with a list of products that need to be redesigned, but the ideas must be **fresh** and **innovative**. The design director gives you a chance to choose **one, or more**, items on the Product List that you are most interested in and would like to explore. Your job is to do some research, generate some ideas, and present your best concepts."

Hand out or write list on the board.
    1- Furniture or beds for a department store. (Comfort)
    2- Sci-Fi monster for a movie. (Fantasy)
    3- Sculpture or fountain for a city park. (Art)
    4- Line of jewelry and/or clothes. (Fashion)
    5- Toy (Fun)
    6- Flashlight (Function)
    7- Idea of the student (approved by the instructor)

wrist light

GENERATE IDEAS
"After choosing your item(s) of interest, do some Springboard Research by going through magazines and cutting out images that will help inspire Visual Thinking, Concept Sketching, and Concept Modeling new ideas. Complete session #9 by finishing your research and doing some initial Concept Sketching, and Modeling. In the next session (#10) bring any new concepts that you thought of after a time of incubation (sleeping on the ideas). Choose and develop your best idea(s) for presentation at the end of the session."

CONCEPT GENERATION HINT
"The client list has descriptive words in parentheses. Try using these or other words to describe different items on the list. Example:
- comfortable sculpture
- functional jewelry
- fun monster
- fantasy flashlight
- artistic furniture
- monster fountain

These, or other descriptive words, help us look at things in a new way."

Clay Sci-fi movie monsters

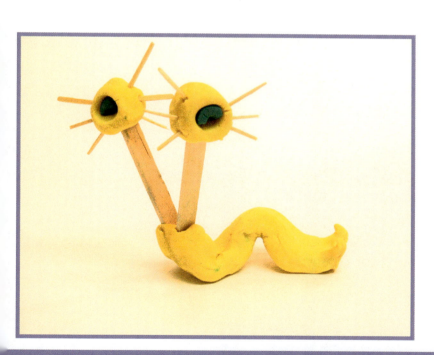

QUOTES

"The convergence of two or more knowledge sets is nesessary for innovation. A new idea happens when two or more seperate thoughts come together in a unique way."
Shira P. White - *New Ideas About New Ideas*

"The best way to have a good idea is to have lots of ideas."
Linus Pauling

"Houston, we have a problem." 11

INTRODUCTION

The astronauts aboard Apollo 13 in April of 1970 would not have made it back to earth if it weren't for the **collaboration** of a number of different people. Like the engineers at Houston, and the astronauts aboard the Apollo, students have **limited** time and materials to brainstorm creative ways to problem solve. The ping-pong ball (or equivalent) in this activity represents a payload that they need to **transport** between each station (desk) using a <u>**different delivery**</u> method for each attempt. (ex. rolling, flying, sliding). They must follow the **rules** for delivery and can only use the materials given. Delivery methods from the list below can be used to **prompt** a greater number of solutions.

Delivery Methods: Push, pull, slide, fly, swing, launch, tether, sling, pole, tube, roll, cable, sail, and others.

Anything goes in this activity, so be open to **wild ideas!** Simply putting the ball in a wadded piece of paper and tossing it to the next station is legitimate.

Supplemental information on the future need for **Creativity**:
• **Ken Robinson** *Out of Our Minds*

fly

QUOTES

"Creativity is not purely an individual performance. It arises out of our interactions with ideas and achievements of other people."
Ken Robinson *Out of Our Minds*

"While ideas are conceived in individual minds, they are seldom born in isolation and rarely realized alone."
Jerry Hirshberg *founder of Nissan Design International*

LESSON

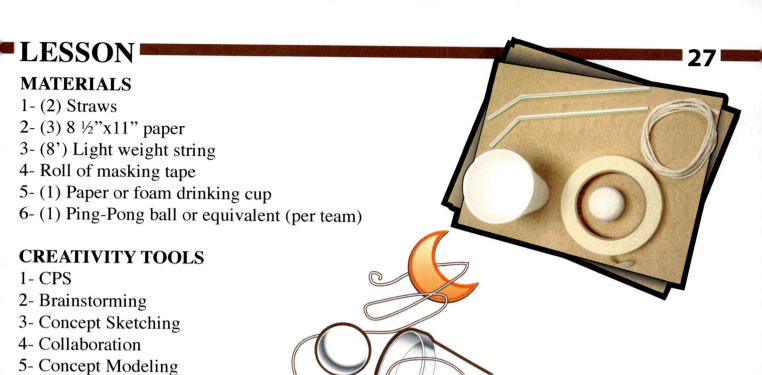

MATERIALS
1- (2) Straws
2- (3) 8 ½"x11" paper
3- (8') Light weight string
4- Roll of masking tape
5- (1) Paper or foam drinking cup
6- (1) Ping-Pong ball or equivalent (per team)

CREATIVITY TOOLS
1- CPS
2- Brainstorming
3- Concept Sketching
4- Collaboration
5- Concept Modeling

TIME
1- Challenge explanation: 5-10 min.
2- Each station brainstorms ways to deliver ping-pong ball (payload): 15 min.
3- Transport payload between stations: 20 min.
4- Discuss and tally delivery methods used by teams: 15 min.

OBJECTIVE
Show students (like the astronauts demonstrated aboard Apollo 13) CPS can be accomplished with limited time and materials.

CHALLENGE
"'Houston, we have a problem'. This was the shocking message from the Apollo 13 spacecraft on its mission to land on the moon. The astronauts needed to solve a malfunction in their equipment quickly in order to return safely to earth. Like the three astronauts on board and the support team in Houston, Texas, your mission is to brainstorm and use creative ways to **problem solve**. Your mission is to transport a payload (Ping-Pong ball) between your desk stations using as many **delivery methods** as possible. Each station will have 15 minutes to brainstorm ideas and 20 minutes to transport the payload as many times as possible between your desks."

RULES
1. (Optional) **No talking**. Communicate only with writing or sketching.
2. Materials can be **shared** between stations.
3. Hands can **never touch** the ball surface directly. Use tape, straw, etc. to handle and move ball around.
4. Ball must be **transported** by a "delivery method." It cannot be simply rolled or thrown on its own.
5. No matter how the payload is delivered it must end up in the **cup** at each station. It then can be moved and sent to the next station.
6. Decide between stations which delivery methods will be used so there is **no duplication** of methods.
7. When sent, the payload must reach the **desk** of the receiving station.
8. **Record** all the different delivery methods in writing or sketches.

ROOM SET-UP
Place desks (stations) 5' apart, 1-3 students at each station, 2-3 stations per team.
See diagram.

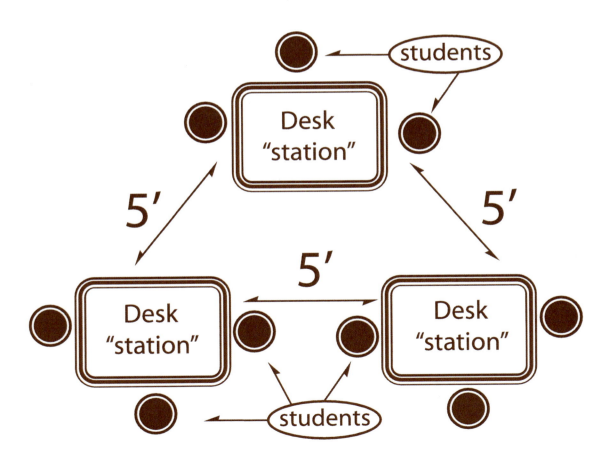

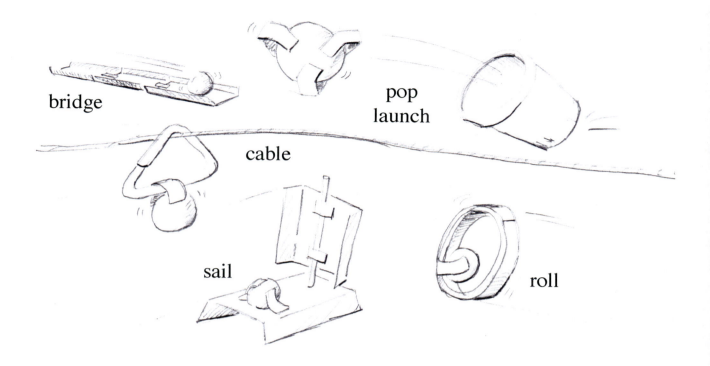

POSSIBLE DELIVERY METHODS

QUOTES

"Much of our educational system has taught us to look for the one right answer. This is fine for some situations, but...often it's the second, or third, or tenth right answer which is what we need to solve a problem in an innovative way."
Roger von Oech - *A Whack on the Side of the Head*

"An effective goal (defined problem) focuses primarily on results rather than activity...it unifies your efforts and energy."
Stephen R. Covey - *The 7 Habits of Highly Effective People*

"Quantity breeds Quality: The more ideas you think up, the more likely you are to arrive at the potentially best leads to solutions."
Alex F. Osborn - *Applied Imagination*

pile of junk 12

INTRODUCTION

In this activity students will begin to apply some of the creativity tools to **everyday problems** and move from the theoretical to more practical applications of creative problem solving.

Students collaborate with one other person, or work by themselves, to develop as many ideas as they can from the **four challenge scenarios**. The last 15 minutes, students will present their best concepts. They will need to go through the four CPS steps when developing their ideas: defining the problem, brainstorming and generating possible solutions, evaluating and choosing the best idea, and implementing the concept.

water bag

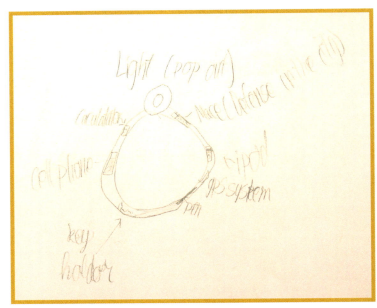

QUOTES

"Novel learning is a critical ingredient of enrichment and contributes to synaptic development and survival."
Eric Jensen *Enriching the Brain*

"To invent you need a good imagination and a pile of junk."
Thomas Edison

LESSON 31

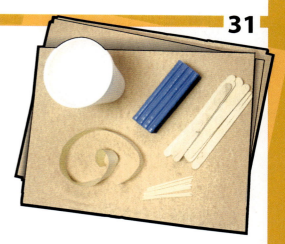

MATERIALS
1- (10) Toothpicks
2- (10) Craft sticks
3- 12" of tape. Extra tape as needed
4- (1) 3oz or 4oz stick of clay
5- Card stock or plain computer paper
6- (1) foam or paper cup

CREATIVITY TOOLS
1- CPS and most of the other creativity tools.

TIME
1- Challenge explanation: 5 min.
2- Develop ideas to solve challenge problems: 30 min.
3- Present favorite product concept: 15 min.

OBJECTIVE
This is an opportunity for students to follow the CPS process and use most of the creativity tools to generate solutions to real world problems.

CHALLENGE
"Now that you have become aware of your great creative potential, its time to look at some **real world problems**, ones that really frustrate people. Your challenge is to identify the problem and generate a number of possible solutions. Then evaluate and choose your best idea, making a sketch and/or model and present your ideas. You have 30 minutes to work on one or more of the problems in the following four scenarios. Be sure to come up with a good name for your product idea."

1- One of the messiest areas of the house is at the front door where a **pile of shoes** seems to accumulate. Everyone has several pairs and often need to sit on the floor to put on boots or tie up sport shoes. Here is an opportunity to design something functional and good-looking.

2- People are often **left in the dark,** with their hands full, when unlocking the car or house door, or working on some equipment in the dark and need both hands free. Invent a device that you don't have to hold that is small, portable, and will shine light where you need it.

3- **Leaf raking** is hard enough, but getting the leaves in the bag is always a great challenge, and often you are alone with no one to hold the bag. Come up with an idea that will make it easier and save time.

4- We are encouraged to drink lots of water, but it's really a hassle to carry around these **bulky plastic containers** that don't easily fit into a pocket, purse or brief case. What concept can you come up with that would be less bulky and more convenient than the existing containers?

uncle Horatio's gift

13

ALL TOOLS used

INTRODUCTION

Much evidence points to the need for continued creative activity throughout our lives, if we are to feel **fulfilled**. Uncle Horatio's Gift offers an opportunity to apply our creativity by designing the perfect "playhouse" we dream of as kids. Fantasy and visual thinking are key in developing a good cabin plan. Sketching and modeling provides an opportunity for those "accidental" discoveries that make for an engaging fun experience. And if we are having fun, we are more likely to seek more creative experiences, for creativity **begets** creativity.

FunThink is all about awakening and strengthening the imaginative spirit that can lead to a lasting creative life style. The **developmental** steps in Uncle Horatio's Gift can be applied to any project, large or small, in which we want to have creative input.

QUOTES

"To a developmental psychologist, the study of creativity is necessarily anchored in the study of human development…If, in the early life, children have the opportunity to discover much about their world and to do so in a comfortable, exploring way, they will accumulate invaluable "capital of creativity" on which they can draw in later life."
Howard Gardener *Creating Minds*

"Older children become more restricted in their creative expression as they are told there is a right and wrong way to do most everything. To maintain your child's natural creative orientation, you need to consciously insure that you provide emotional and intellectual support for novel ideas and behavior."
William H. Staso, PhD *Promoting Creativity*

LESSON

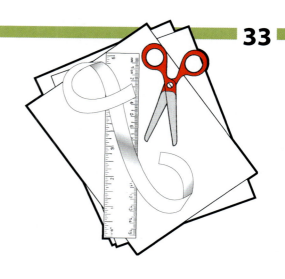

MATERIALS *(per person)*
1- (3) 8½"x11" sheets card stock or equivalent light-weight poster board
2- 24" Masking tape
3- Sketch paper
4- Ruler
5- Scissors

CREATIVITY TOOLS
1- All 12 creativity tools

TIME
First Period
1- Challenge explanation: 5 min.
2- Students copy and discuss Mind Map cabin plan: 10 min.
3- Concept Sketch cabin ideas: 35 min.

Second Period
1- Challenge explanation: 5 min.
2- Draw cabin floorplan: 30 min.
3- Draw your cabin on the property with landscaping ideas: 15 min.

Third Period
1- Challenge explanation: 5 min.
2- Concept Model the cabin: 30 min.
3- Draw your cabin on the property in a perspective view: 15 min.

OBJECTIVE
Learn the natural flow of a project development plan.

cabin concept sketch

First Period Challenge

"Your great uncle Horatio Hilton has left you a spectacular piece of property over looking beautiful Lake Tahoe. The five acres are punctuated with tall pines and supple aspen trees with a winding, gurgling brook flowing to a pebbled beach. Along with the property comes $200,000 in cash with the stipulation that you design and build the cabin yourself, which will be used as a retreat for you and your family. Also you must agree not to have any electronic devices in the cabin, and have only one phone to use in case of emergencies. To get you off to a good start, your uncle left a Mind Map plan to help you generate ideas for your cabin. Your first challenge is to sketch some cabin designs. Using the Mind Map, think about the elements that go into making a great cabin.

Cabin Mind Map Plan and Sketches

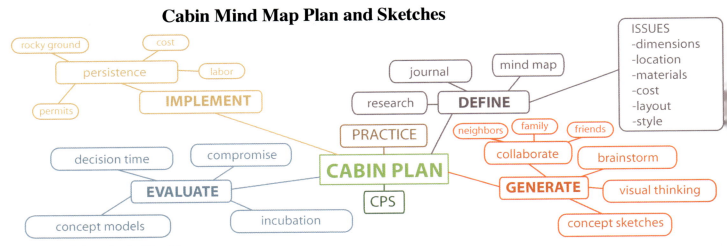

Second Period Challenge

"Now that you have some sketches of your cabin, translate them into a floor plan showing the layout and size of the rooms: bedrooms, bath, kitchen, etc. Remember, this is your design so do whatever you desire. (Instructor could show a sample floor plan on the board.) When you have completed the layout, draw your five-acre property on Lake Tahoe and place your cabin on it. Add all the details around it you want: trees, boulders, decks, dock, etc.

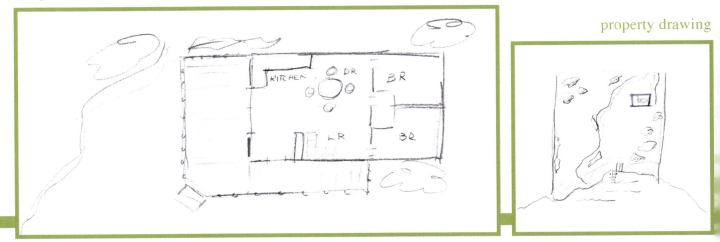

sample floor plan

property drawing

Third Period Challenge
"Now for the final challenge. Using only poster board and tape, make a simple model of your cabin design. Using scissors, pencil and a ruler, cut out your model, adding any features you want: windows, doors, chimney, etc. If you have time, draw a perspective view of your cabin as it sits on the property.

perspective drawing

concept model

QUOTES

"I have been finding in all my clinical work that many aspects of contemporary life can stunt the growth of key neurodevelopmental functions… Schools that are highly and tightly structured so that there is little time for original thinking can (also) short circuit brainstorming in students."
Mel Levine, M.D. *A Mind at a Time*

"I'm convinced that if you participate regularly in brainstormers, it's like stretching exercises for your mind. Doodling, drawing, modeling. Sketch ideas and make things, and you're likely to encourage accidental discoveries. At the most fundamental level, what we're talking about is play, about exploring borders."
Tom Kelly *The Art of Innovation*

FUNthink conclusion 14

ALL TOOLS used

REFLECTION

The Funthink concept is about **curious exploration,** and using our knowledge and innate creativity to spark Creative Problem Solving. The thesaurus definition of fun and think further illuminates the concept.

fun *adj* enjoyable, interesting, entertaining, agreeable, pleasurable, playful, lighthearted, pleasing, amusing.
think *verb* reflect, ponder, consider, deliberate, judge, estimate, contemplate, concentrate, reason, recall, image, visualize, dream.

Keeping the expanded definition in mind will help to **broaden** the understanding and use of the Creativity Tools. The principles of CPS have been validated by the research of the **Lemelson Center for the Study of Invention and Innovation**. Ideo, America's leading design firm credited for thousands of innovative products, puts them into practical use. Famous creators like Thomas Edison and Walt Disney have also used these principles.

Creativity Tools can be used in analyzing and solving **daily problems** that are met in our home, community and work life. Understanding and using the tools helps us approach a goal or problem with greater confidence. Once we experience and trust our own creative inclinations, we feel more engaged in whatever activity we pursue.

QUOTES

"Prototyping (concept sketching/modeling) doesn't just solve straight forward problems… once you start drawing or making things, you open up new possibilities of discovery."
Tom Kelley *The Art of Innovation*

"The intuitive mind is a sacred gift and the rational mind is a faithful servant. We have created a society that honors the servant and has forgotten the gift."
Albert Einstein

(*continued from previous page*)

In my creative life at home, my wife and I use the Creativity Tools in developing set designs for a community theater, or skits for our Sunday school class. My granddaughters and I will use many of the Tools in designing and building a backyard **playhouse** this coming summer, using scrap and reclaimed lumber.

As a clay sculptor for a motor sports company, I use CPS in **translating** sketches into full-size models for the design department.

As an **inventor,** my favorite subject is developing toys, wooden puzzles, and games. While going through the ideation process, I will use all the Creativity Tools at one time or another. For example, I might pose a goal of developing a new building block concept and then brainstorm ideas using concept sketches and quick concept models. I have come to realize that getting materials in hand and ideas on paper is needed to seed further development of a concept. Without these first simple **visual recordings** of my subjectthoughts I could not get any further then the opening goal statement.

Through the **manipulation** of sketches and blocks, new possibilities unfold. The ideas that hold the most promise will be tested on family and friends to gain feedback. More sketches, models, incubation, research, journaling, collaboration, and brainstorming, brings me closer to a final concept. Once I get that "this feels right" feeling, a final prototype is built and either submitted to a toy company for possible licensing, or shelved for further development after more incubation.

The best advice I can give to those who want to be good problem solvers is to keep a **sketchbook journal**. Date each entry, be it a sketch, doodle or thought. Practice visual thinking, sketching and mind mapping your ideas, plans and future. Any problem, large or small, can be tackled given the proper background knowledge and creative thinking.

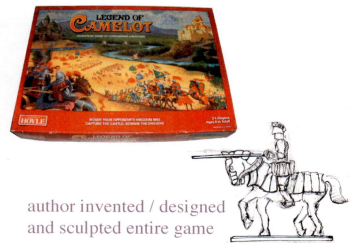

author invented / designed and sculpted entire game

38

Crossbows and Catapults invented by author sold over 1,000,000 games worldwide

QUOTES

"There is nothing in a caterpillar that tells you that it's going to be a butterfly."
Buckminster Fuller - *Inventor*

"When I am working on a problem I never think about beauty. I only think about how to solve the probem."
Buckminster Fuller - *Inventor*

"Creativity is not neat and orderly. It is not organized."
Shira P. White - *New Ideas About New Ideas*

LESSON

MATERIALS
1- All previous materials should be made available at a central location.

CREATIVITY TOOLS
1- Students are free to use any of the creativity tools they need to get desired results.

TIME
1- After the challenge statement is read, students use remaining time to work on their stated goal or problem.

OBJECTIVE
The key to a successful solution is a well-stated and understood problem/goal. So on to the ultimate challenge where the student will come up with their own goal or problem statement and develop a good solution using the Creativity Tools they have acquired.

CHALLENGE
"The final challenge is for you to generate a goal or problem statement and then develop a solution using the creativity tools. Following are some ideas to spark your imagination, or come up with your own topic.
- Mind map a short story about a funny family incident or misadventure.
- Interview a grandparent or other family member using the "Scoop" interview form.
- Develop a concept that will solve a problem of something that really bugs you.
- Take another look at the Product List in chapter #9 and #10 for ideas.
- New concepts for transportation, housing, or energy.

Upon completion, present your goal/problem and solution (in writing or through demonstration), stating the various creativity tools used.

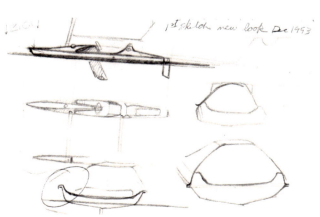

TriSailer - concept sketch and finished product invented and patented by author

FUNTHINK AFTERWORD

In the 50's my family would often travel by car from Michigan to Fresno, California to visit my older sister and her family. On a return trip, when I was eight, my sister insightfully prepared a shoebox for me half-full of stuff you might find in a kitchen junk drawer: rubber bands, tape, toothpicks, string, paper clips, etc. These trips often took five days, driving route 66, giving me plenty of time to explore the contents of that box. Thinking back, I now believe that was the beginning of my becoming an inventor and designer.

I don't actually recall what I made -- just that it kept me occupied the entire trip, as there was always something new in that box to make. The shoebox might be analogous to a blank canvas, or page in a sketchbook; the possibilities are endless.

The core idea behind FunThink came from that experience. I have learned since then that it isn't so important what medium is used, as that we are able to express ourselves creatively. I am convinced that to feel fulfilled, we all need to find our personal method of creative expression, be it sewing, dancing, planning a school program, solving community problems, or whatever.

QUOTE

"Happiness is not in the mere possession of money; it lies in the joy of achievement, in the thrill of creative effort."
Franklin D. Roosevelt

worksheet  41

#2 "DESIGNER ISLAND" DEVELOPMENT PLAN

Island Description for "Bird's Eye View" Sketch: abundant wild life, fruited tropical plants, coral reefs teeming with fish, lush green forest, fertile valleys, storm-safe harbors, and crystal-clear fresh water steams that flow from cloud- haloed mineral-rich mountains.

Organize Community: When answering the questions below, show how you will **lay out and organize** your new-found home by sketching the island outline and filling in the areas of development on the 11"x17" page. Considering what you know from the present and what you have observed from the future, how will you provide for the long-term needs (next 100 years) of your community while maintaining the natural beauty and ecological balance of your new-found home?

*How will you shelter, feed, and clothe everyone?

*What will you do to provide health care, education, recreation, and transportation?

*What steps will you take to maintain the natural beauty and ecological balance on this island?

****

If time permits consider the following:
    Government
    Economy
    Exploration
    Manufacturing
    Mining
    Lumbering
    Waste Management
    Shipping
    Power
    Culture

worksheet  43

#4 SCOOP INTERVIEW FORM

Research Questions
1- When and where were you **born**?
2- Give me some information about your **family**.
3- Tell me about your favorite **vacation**.
4- What do you do with your **free time**?
5- What kind of **food** do you fix for yourself and or family?
6- What do you see yourself doing at age **30, age 80**?
7- If you were in charge of a **charity fund** who would you help and how?
8- Tell me something **about yourself** that people may not know.

Mind Map

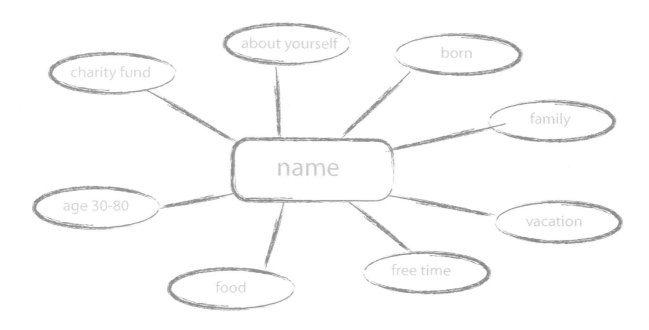

Article

worksheet  **45**

worksheet 51

trace first, then copy second

worksheet  53

REVIEW OF CREATIVITY TOOLS FOR #6

Choose the correct order for Creative Problem Solving (number 1-4):
 Evaluate and select best solution ____.
 Implement and demonstrate best solution____.
 Define the problem or goal____.
 Generate a number of possible solutions____.

 Fill in the blank with the correct creative tool from list below.

1- Continue to press on in spite of difficulty _____
2- Generate creative ways to meet a goal or solve a problem. _____
3- Use simple sketches to manipulate ideas on paper. _____
4- Record experiences to be used later in problem solving. _____
5- Allowing the subconscious to work on problems: "sleep on it" _____
6- Background information used to help problem solve. _____
7- Repeated activity to gain and maintain a skill. _____
8- Use your "minds eye" to work on problems in your head. _____
9- Work with others to generate ideas and problem solve. _____
10- A graphic method of organizing information. _____
11- Use simple model materials to explore concepts. _____

A- Brainstorming
B- Visual Thinking
C- Concept Sketching
D- Concept Modeling
E- Journaling
F- Mind Mapping
G- Collaboration
H- Incubation
I- Springboard Research
J- Persistence
K- Practice

Made in the USA
Middletown, DE
19 August 2019